# *Spirituality*
## Passages in Search of
## the Heart of God

# *Spirituality*

## Passages in Search of the Heart of God

Edited by Jude Patterson

BARNES
&NOBLE
BOOKS
NEW YORK

Compilation copyright © 2003 by Barnes & Noble, Inc.

2003 Barnes & Noble Books

ISBN 0-7607-4074-7

Printed and bound in the United States of America

M 9 8 7 6 5 4 3 2 1

*To Amma Suzanne*
*with deepest gratitude*

*The Soul should always stand ajar.*

—EMILY DICKINSON

## INTRODUCTION

MYSTICISM IS THE HUMAN SOUL'S DIRECT EXPERIENCE of ultimate reality, a deep communion between the individual and the Supreme Being. Mysticism is to religion as creativity is to art: an attempt to climb inside of the essence or heart of the form, to find oneself at one with that heart, and to share with the world the gifts emanating from the experience. In describing their journey to God, many mystics liken the sublime joy that comes from divine union to the ecstasy of Love shared between Lover and Beloved. Yet this deeply personal relationship with God is not the domain of a chosen few, but is within the reach of all who seek it, for God's love pervades the universe. As the poet Tennyson said, "Closer is He than breathing, / and nearer than hands and feet."

Our minds fumble about with language to describe a plane of reality that is beyond speech. Even the name God can serve only as a symbol for so great a Mystery. Theologians traditionally use the pronoun *He* for God, *man* for a being with a body and a soul, and *she* for the soul and the created realm, the art of God, called nature. The English language has not yet evolved eloquent replacements that suitably describe the God who is not only beyond gender, color, creed, and politics, but beyond language itself. The divine language of silence, contemplation of the mysteries of God, and knowing by unknowing are the doors upon which the mystics knock. Each of us is a mystic whenever we daydream about God.

A recurring metaphor for entering on this cosmic journey is that of the doorway, the dark corridor, the mystic ladder into the heart of God. The word *passages* in the title refers therefore not only to the corridors, doorways, and ladders traversed by pilgrim souls who have pined for God, but also the textual passages extracted from their writings and gathered here. May the light beams shining from the lamps of these fellow travelers illuminate your soul's path and inspire your heart's heavenly daydreams.

—*Jude Patterson*

# The Waking
# Heart

On the threshold between dream and life, sleep and waking, and darkness and sunshine, we find a special doorway to the spiritual and the eternal.

—THOMAS MOORE

Even as a man who is asleep awakes, but when he is asleep does not know that he is going to awake, so a part of the subtle invisible Spirit comes as a messenger to the body without the body being conscious of his arrival.... This Spirit is consciousness and gives consciousness to the body: he is the driver of the chariot.

—UPANISHADS

When the thought of thee wakes in our hearts let it not awaken like a frightened bird that flies about in dismay, but like a child waking from its sleep with a heavenly smile.

—SØREN KIERKEGAARD

How much did I hear of religion as a child? Very little, and yet my heart leaped when I heard the name of God. I do believe every soul has a tendency toward God.

—DOROTHY DAY

From childhood on I have had the dream of life lived as a sacrament.... The dream implied taking life ritually as something holy.

—BERNARD BERENSON

The spirituality of my childhood is the one I would most like to have restored. It was pure and fresh and honest. I read God everywhere!

—MACRINA WIEDERKEHR

The fullness of joy is to behold God in everything.

—JULIAN OF NORWICH

God is a sea of infinite substance.

—JOHN OF DAMASCUS

Because you cannot see him, God is everywhere.

—YASUNARI KAWABATA

God, I can push the grass apart
And lay my finger on Thy heart.

—EDNA ST. VINCENT MILLAY

Every crystal, every flower a window opening into heaven, a mirror reflecting the Creator.

—JOHN MUIR

Nature is the glass reflecting God.

—EDWARD YOUNG

Nature has some perfections to show that she is the image of God, and some defects to show that she is only His image.

—BLAISE PASCAL

Nature is but a name for an effect,
Whose cause is God.

—WILLIAM COWPER

The whole of creation, with all its laws, is a revelation of God.

—WILLIAM RALPH INGE

As a house implies a builder, and a garment a weaver, and a door a carpenter, so does the existence of the Universe imply a Creator.

—AKIBA BEN JOSEPH

I think that the leaf of a tree, the meanest insect on which we trample, are in themselves arguments more conclusive than any which can be adduced that some vast intellect animates Infinity.

—PERCY BYSSHE SHELLEY

Whoever it was who searched the heavens with a telescope and found no God would not have found the human mind if he had searched the brain with a microscope.

—GEORGE SANTAYANA

We need no ladders to the sky, we need only...
observe the structure and functions of man's bodily organs,... to know that the Creator exists. Job said, "From my flesh shall I see God."

—Abba Mari ben Eligdor

I could prove God statistically. Take the human body alone—the chances that all the functions of an individual would just happen is a statistical monstrosity.

—George H. Gallup

Nothing is accidental in the universe—that is one of my Laws of Physics—except the entire universe itself, which is Pure Accident, pure divinity.

—Joyce Carol Oates

The extent of the whole universe is but a point, an atom, compared to His immensity.

—JEAN DE LA BRUYÉRE

God is the tangential point between zero and infinity.

—ALFRED JARRY

[God is] a circle whose center is everywhere and circumference nowhere.

—TIMAEUS OF LOCRIS

No statement about God is simply, literally true. God is far more than can be measured, described, defined in ordinary language, or pinned down to any particular happening.

—DAVID JENKINS

It is as impossible for man to demonstrate the existence of God as it would be for even Sherlock Holmes to demonstrate the existence of Arthur Conan Doyle.

—FREDERICK BUECHNER

We need God, not in order to understand the *why,* but in order to feel and sustain the ultimate *wherefore,* to give a meaning to the universe.

—MIGUEL DE UNAMUNO

Faith consists in being vitally concerned with that ultimate reality to which I give the symbolical name of God. Whoever reflects earnestly on the meaning of life is on the verge of an act of faith.

—PAUL TILLICH

God does not die on the day when we cease to believe in a personal deity, but we die on the day when our lives cease to be illumined by the steady radiance, renewed daily, of a wonder, the source of which is beyond all reason.

—DAG HAMMARSKJÖLD

Wonder and knowledge are both to be cherished. Shall we appreciate any less the beauty of nature because its harmony is unplanned? And shall the potential of mind cease to inspire our awe and fear because several billion neurons reside in our skulls?

—STEPHEN JAY GOULD

Physical science has limited its scope so as to leave a background which we are at liberty to, or even invited to, fill with a reality of spiritual import.

—ARTHUR STANLEY EDDINGTON

Science is not only compatible with spirituality; it is a profound source of spirituality.

—CARL SAGAN

The cosmic religious experience is the strongest force and the noblest driving force behind scientific research.

—ALBERT EINSTEIN

Science and religion ... are two sides of the same glass, through which we see darkly until these two, focusing together, reveal the truth.

—PEARL S. BUCK

Religion is as necessary to reason as reason is to religion. The one cannot exist without the other.

—GEORGE WASHINGTON

Reason is our soul's left hand, Faith her right,
By these we reach divinity.

—JOHN DONNE

It is the heart which perceives God and not the reason. That is what faith is: God perceived by the heart, not by the reason.

—BLAISE PASCAL

If it can be verified, we don't need faith.... Faith is for that which lies on the *other* side of reason. Faith is what makes life bearable, with all its tragedies and ambiguities and sudden, startling joys.

—MADELEINE L'ENGLE

The living God is related to the categories and formal arguments of our abstract thinking as fire is related to paper.

—ARTHUR VOGEL

Thinking gives off smoke to prove the existence of fire. A mystic sits inside the burning.

—RUMI

In mysticism,...the attempt is given up to know God by thought, and it is replaced by the experience of union with God in which there is no more room—and no need—for knowledge *about* God.

—ERICH FROMM

The most beautiful emotion we can experience is the mystical.... To know that what is impenetrable to us really exists, manifesting itself as the highest wisdom and the most radiant beauty, which our dull faculties can comprehend only in primitive form—this knowledge, this feeling, is at the center of true religiousness.

—ALBERT EINSTEIN

The mysteries of faith are degraded if they are made into an object of affirmation and negation, when in reality they should be an object of contemplation.

—Simone Weil

I am ... reminded of the humility of those early theologians who knew that when we seek to speak of God, we do so only out of the glimmers of understanding that sparkle amid the vast background of uncomprehended mystery, a mystery that nevertheless shines in nature and in the human spirit with unquenchable light.

—Robert J. Russell

At the back of our brains, so to speak, there is a forgotten blaze or burst of astonishment at our own existence. The object of the artistic and spiritual life is to dig for this submerged sunrise of wonder.

—G. K. Chesterton

The mystical life is the centre of all that I do & all that I think & all that I write.... I have always considered myself a voice of what I believe to be a greater renaissance—the revolt of the soul against the intellect.

—WILLIAM BUTLER YEATS

The soul itself, the soul of each one of us, is to each one of us a mystery. It hides in the dark and broods, and consciousness cannot tell us of its workings.

—OSCAR WILDE

They will question you concerning the soul. Say: "The soul is the concern of my Lord, and you have been given of knowledge but a little."

—QUR'AN

God has plans which mortals don't understand. He rests in the womb when the new baby forms. Whispers the life dream to infinitesimal cells. It is God who lies under the thoughts of man. He is cartilage. Memory.

—ELLEASE SOUTHERLAND

God is the *mysterium tremendum* that appears and overthrows, but he is also the mystery of the self-evident, nearer to me than my I.

—MARTIN BUBER

I was a hidden treasure; I wished to be known; therefore I created the world.

—MUHAMMAD

And the Lord God formed man of the dust of the ground, and breathed into his nostrils the breath of life; and man became a living soul.

—Genesis 2:7

The life whereby we are joined into the body is called the soul.... Just as the soul is the life of the body, so God is the life of the soul.

—Augustine of Hippo

The human soul is a silent harp in God's quire, whose strings need only to be swept by the divine breath to chime in with the harmonies of creation.

—Henry David Thoreau

Every soul is a melody which needs renewing.

—Stéphane Mallarmé

No human soul is like any other human soul, and therefore the love of God for any human soul is infinite, for no other soul can satisfy the same need in God.

—WILLIAM BUTLER YEATS

Every friendship with God and every love between Him and a soul is the *only one* of its kind.

—JANET ERSKINE STUART

Faith is the marriage of God and the Soul.

—JOHN OF THE CROSS

The unfathomable mystery of God is that God is a Lover who wants to be loved.

HENRI J. M. NOUWEN

Wouldest thou wit thy Lord's meaning in this thing? Wit it well: Love was his meaning. Who shewed it thee? Love. What shewed He thee? Love. Wherefore shewed it He? for Love.... Thus was I learned that Love is our Lord's meaning.

—JULIAN OF NORWICH

You made us for yourself, and our hearts find no peace until they rest in you.

—AUGUSTINE OF HIPPO

It is only through love that we can attain to communion with God. All living knowledge of God rests upon this foundation: that we experience Him in our lives as Will-to-Love.

—ALBERT SCHWEITZER

Without love the Self cannot hold together.... There can be knowledge, intellect, genius even: but without love there is not integration.

—P. W. Martin

Search and discover the root of your soul, so that you can fulfill it and restore it to its source, its essence. The more you fulfill yourself, the closer you approach your authentic self.

—Kabbalah

God expects but one thing of you, and that is that you ... let God be God in you.

—Meister Eckhart

God, being unable to effect His purposes without hands and brains, has made us evolve our hands and brains to act and think for Him: in short, we are not in the hands of God; but God is in our hands.

—GEORGE BERNARD SHAW

Nature uses human imagination to lift her work of creation to even higher levels.

—LUIGI PIRANDELLO

I think human beings are the superior sentient beings on this planet. Humans have the potential not only to create happy lives for themselves, but also to help other beings. We have a natural creative ability and it is very important to realize this.

—DALAI LAMA

The fierce power of imagination is a gift from God. Joined with the grandeur of the mind, the potency of inference, ethical depth, and the natural sense of the divine, imagination becomes an instrument for the holy spirit.

—KABBALAH

Imagination is the eye of the soul.

—JOSEPH JOUBER

Those who know him who is the eye of the eye, the ear of the ear, the mind of the mind and the life of life, they know Brahman from the beginning of time.

—UPANISHADS

The soul is partly in eternity and partly in time.

—MARSILIO FICINO

The soul is not like God: she is identical with Him.

—MEISTER ECKHART

Sin is whatever obscures the soul.

—ANDRÉ GIDE

Man is free whenever he produces or manifests God, and through this he becomes immortal.

—FRIEDRICH VON SCHLEGEL

Man is the link between God and Nature.... As God has descended into man, so man must ascend to God.

—JILI

Just as man was once revealed out of God, so, when the circle closes, God may be revealed out of man.

—CARL JUNG

History is a vision of God's creation on the move.

—ARNOLD J. TOYNBEE

The spiritual life does not remove us from the world but leads us deeper into it.

—HENRI J. M. NOUWEN

Within the province of our ephemeral flesh all of God is imperiled. He cannot be saved unless we save him with our own struggles, nor can we be saved unless he is saved. We are one.

—NIKOS KAZANTZAKIS

Religion points to that area of human experience where in one way or another man comes upon mystery as a summons to pilgrimage.

—FREDERICK BUECHNER

The only journey is the journey within.

—RAINER MARIA RILKE

Communion with the transcendent powers ... is not a feat that can be achieved by anyone; it is a mystery peculiar to the one elected, and is therefore through and through personal in character.

—THEODORE ROSZAK

Religion consists in the simple feeling of a relationship of dependence upon something above us and a desire to establish relations with this mysterious power.

—MIGUEL DE UNAMUNO

Religion is born when we accept the ultimate frustration of mere human effort, and at the same time realize the strength which comes from union with superhuman reality.

—JOHN BUCHAN

I hope to improve myself. I do not know how to, but I feel that God will help all those who seek him.

—VASLAV NIJINSKY

How can I be useful, of what service can I be?
There is something inside me, what can it be?

—Vincent van Gogh

There is nothing I want to find out and long to
know with greater urgency than this. Can I find
God, whom I can almost grasp with my own hands
in looking at the universe, also in myself?

—Johannes Keple

# The Vale of
# Soul-Making

Brooding on God, I may become a man.
Pain wanders through my bones like a lost fire;
What burns me now? Desire, desire, desire.

—THEODORE ROETHKE

I loved not, yet I loved to love ... I sought what I
might love, loving to love.

—AUGUSTINE OF HIPPO

Longing is the core of mystery.
Longing itself brings the cure.
The only rule is, *Suffer the pain.*

—RUMI

St. Teresa of Avila described our life in this world
as like a night at a second-class hotel

—MALCOLM MUGGERIDGE

Call the world if you please "the vale of soul-making." Then you will find out the use of the world.

—JOHN KEATS

The search is for the living God, the creative ground of all we are and can become. Only "in spirit and in truth," the whole-hearted devotion fundamental both to religion and to science, can it be undertaken.

—P. W. MARTIN

The action of the creative individual may be described as a twofold motion of withdrawal-and-return: withdrawal for the purpose of his personal enlightenment, return for the task of enlightening his fellow men.

—ARNOLD J. TOYNBEE

The ultimate aim of the quest ... must be neither release nor ecstasy for oneself, but wisdom and power to serve others.

—JOSEPH CAMPBELL

Human service is the highest form of self-interest.

—ELBERT HUBBARD

It is by forgetting self that one finds self.

—FRANCIS OF ASSISI

We cannot be filled unless we are first emptied, to make room for what is to come.

—THOMAS MERTON

Humility is the root of love. Humility exerts an irresistible power upon God.

—Simone Weil

There is no good in trying to be more spiritual than God. God never means man to be a purely spiritual creature.... He likes matter. He created it.

—C. S. Lewis

The *Thou* meets me through grace—it is not found by seeking.

—Martin Buber

The daily bread of grace, without which nothing can be achieved, is given to the extent to which we ourselves give and forgive.

—Aldous Huxley

Since nothing we intend is ever faultless, and nothing we attempt ever without error, and nothing we achieve without some measure of finitude and fallibility we call humanness, we are saved by forgiveness.

—David Augsburger

The breeze of God's grace is blowing continually. You have to set your sail to catch that breeze.

—Swami Prabhavananda

Prayer is your open line to God, who is the giver of all gifts.

—Russell W. Lake

Prayer is an invitation to God to intervene in our lives.

—Abraham Joshua Heschel

It's not enough just to sit down and then, with a totally mundane motivation, proceed into meditation. Rather,... it is necessary to bring forth a virtuous motivation, specifically the spirit of awakening for the sake of all sentient beings.

—Padmasambhava

Whether we sit with our arms folded this way and our legs crossed that way is of little consequence. But it is extremely important to check and see if whatever meditation we do is an actual remedy for our suffering.

—Lama Thubten Yeshe

We need to find God, and he cannot be found in noise and restlessness. God is the friend of silence. See how nature—trees, flowers, grass—grows in silence; see the stars, the moon and the sun, how they move in silence.... We need silence to be able to touch souls.

—MOTHER TERESA

For the Great Spirit is everywhere; He hears whatever is in our minds and hearts, and it is not necessary to speak to Him in a loud voice.

—BLACK ELK

There are no waves in the depths of the sea: it is still, unbroken. It is the same with the monk. He is still, without any quiver of desire, without a remnant on which to build pride and desire.

—PALI TRIPITAKA

Emptiness is not a negative state; it denotes a mind that has no tension, no worry or fear, and is wide open to see the Dharma within. Such a mind has let go of all preconceived ideas about the world and the people in it. If our ideas up to now have not brought total and absolute happiness, it is much better to let go of them and be an empty vessel into which the Dharma can be poured. As the Dharma fills us, it changes our outlook and eventually brings us to right view.

—AYYA KHEMA

I am the vessel. The draft is God's. And God is the thirsty one.

—DAG HAMMARSKJÖLD

Our need of Him is but an echo of His need of us.

—ABRAHAM JOSHUA HESCHEL

I strain toward God; God strains toward me. I ache for God; God aches for me. Prayer is mutual yearning, mutual straining, mutual aching.

—MACRINA WIEDERKEHR

Prayer is the soul's sincere desire,
uttered or unexpressed;
the motion of a hidden fire
that trembles in the breast.

—JAMES MONTGOMERY

Contemplation is naught else than a secret, peaceful and loving infusion from God, which, if it be permitted, enkindles the soul with the spirit of love.

—JOHN OF THE CROSS

Prayer oneth the soul to God.

—JULIAN OF NORWICH

Prayer is the air Christ breathes.

—UNKNOWN

Speak to Him, thou, for He hears,
and Spirit with Spirit can meet—
Closer is He than breathing,
and nearer than hands and feet.

—ALFRED, LORD TENNYSON

Just as in earthly life lovers long for the moment
when they are able to breathe forth their love for
each other, to let their souls blend in a soft whis-
per, so the mystic longs for the moment when in
prayer he can, as it were, creep into God.

—SØREN KIERKEGAARD

This is thy hour, O Soul, thy flight into the
     wordless,
Away from books, away from art, the day erased,
     the lesson done,
Thee fully forth emerging, silent, gazing,
     pondering the themes thou lovest best,
Night, sleep, death and the stars.

—WALT WHITMAN

O my Lord, the stars are shining and the eyes of
men are closed, and kings have shut their doors
and every lover is alone with his beloved, and
here am I alone with Thee.

—RABI'A

When you close your doors, and make darkness
within, remember never to say that you are alone,
for you are not alone; nay, God is within, and
your genius is within. And what need have they of
light to see what you are doing?

—EPICTETUS

But when the self speaks to the self, who is speaking?—the entombed soul, the spirit driven in, in, in to the central catacomb; the self that took the veil and left the world—a coward perhaps, yet somehow beautiful, as it flits with its lantern restlessly up and down the dark corridors.

—Virginia Woolf

I throw myself down in my chamber, and I call in, and invite God, and his Angels thither, and when they are there, I neglect God and his Angels, for the noise of a fly, for the rattling of a coach, for the whining of a door.

—John Donne

Although I try
to hold the single thought of Buddha's teaching
    in my heart,
I cannot help but hear
the many crickets' voices calling as well.

—Izumi Shikibu

Whoever delves into mysticism cannot help but stumble, as it is written: "This stumbling block is in your hand." You cannot grasp these things unless you stumble over them.

—Kabbalah

There are very few human beings who receive the truth, complete and staggering, by instant illumination. Most of them acquire it fragment by fragment, on a small scale, by successive developments, cellularly, like a laborious mosaic.

—Anaïs Nin

The brighter and the more manifest in themselves are supernatural things the darker are they to our understanding.

—John of the Cross

Two prisoners whose cells adjoin communicate with each other by knocking on the wall. The wall is the thing which separates them but is also their means of communication. It is the same with us and God. Every separation is a link.

—SIMONE WEIL

Yet it is in our idleness, our dreams, that the submerged truth sometimes comes to the top.

—VIRGINIA WOOLF

The most godly knowing of God is that which is known by unknowing.

—DIONYSIUS OF PARIS

God secludes Himself; but the thinker listens at the door.

—VICTOR HUGO

The Soul should always stand ajar.

—EMILY DICKINSON

He comes to the thought of those who know him beyond thought, not to those who imagine he can be attained by thought: he is unknown to the learned, and known to the simple.

—UPANISHADS

I have one small drop
of knowing in my soul. Let it dissolve in your
    ocean.

—RUMI

To think of God is not to find Him as an object in our minds but to find ourselves in Him.

—ABRAHAM JOSHUA HESCHEL

Moonlight and the sound of pines are things we
    all know,
Zen mind and delusion distinguish sage
    and fool.
Go back to the place where not one thought
    appears;
how shall I put this into words for you?

—HAN-SHAN TE-CH'ING

There is a voice that
doesn't use words. Listen
to that as your personal self breaks open....
    Hear the ecstatic
dumbness inside poetry and discourses on
    mystery. For
*one* day try *not* speaking!

—RUMI

Do not the most moving moments of our lives find us all without words?

—Marcel Marceau

Silence is the language of God.

—Swami Shivananda

The learning of the grammar of silence is an art much more difficult to learn than the grammar of sounds.

—Ivan Illich

Silence [is] the unbearable repartee.

—Alexander Theroux

Prayer is not hearing yourself talk, but being silent, staying silent and waiting until you hear God.

—SØREN KIERKEGAARD

Let a man return into his own self, and there in the centre of his soul, let him wait upon God, as one who listens to another speaking from a high tower, as though he had God in his heart, as though in the whole creation there was only God and his soul.

—PETER OF ALCÁNTARA

The Buddha is as near to you as your own heart.

—AYYA KHEMA

In the silence of the heart God speaks. If you face God in prayer and silence, God will speak to you. Then you will know that you are nothing. It is only when you realize your nothingness, your emptiness, that God can fill you with Himself. Souls of prayer are souls of great silence.

—MOTHER TERESA

When you train yourself to hear the voice of God in everything, you attain the quintessence of the human spirit.

—KABBALAH

Where is God? In the heart of everyone who seeks Him.

—ABRAHAM BEN SAMUEL CHASDAI

Truly do I exist in all beings, but I am most manifest in man. The human heart is my favorite dwelling-place.

—SRIMAD BHAGAVATAM

Be still, and know that I am God.

—PSALM 46:10

He that loveth not knoweth not God: for God is love.

—1 JOHN 4:8

By love he knows me in truth, who I am and what I am. And when he knows me in truth he enters into my Being.

—BHAGAVAD GITA

When you have succeeded in enshrining God within your heart, you will see Him everywhere.

—SWAMI SHIVANANDA

You should not say, "God is in my heart," but rather, "I am in the heart of God."

—KAHLIL GIBRAN

We are no longer alone, for we find that our innermost self is the spirit, that it is God, the indivisible. And suddenly we find ourselves in the midst of the world, yet undisturbed by its multiplicity, for in our innermost soul we know ourselves to be one with all being.

—HERMANN HESSE

If
anyone asks you to say who you
are, say without hesitation,
*soul within soul within soul.* . . .
        Going in search of
the heart, I found a huge rose
under my feet, and roses under
all our feet *!*. . .
Everything is soul and flowering.

—RUMI

Accustomed long to contemplating Love and
Compassion, I have forgotten all difference
between myself and others.

—MILAREPA

Who sees all beings in his own Self, and his own Self in all beings, loses all fear. When a sage sees this great Unity and his Self has become all beings, what delusion and what sorrow can ever be near him?

—UPANISHADS

This identity out of the One into the One and with the One is the source and fountainhead and breaking forth of glowing Love.

—MEISTER ECKHART

He who loves God loves all.

—GOTTFRIED LEIBNIZ

Love begets love. This torment is my joy.

—THEODORE ROETHKE

In the faces of men and women I see God, and
in my own face in the glass,
I find letters from God dropt in the street, and
every one is sign'd by God's name.
And I leave them where they are, for I know
that wheresoe'er I go,
Others will punctually come for ever and ever.

—WALT WHITMAN

"Pass in, pass in," the angels say,
"In to the upper doors,
Nor count compartments of the floors,
But mount to paradise
By the stairway of surprise."

—RALPH WALDO EMERSON

God changes his appearance every second. Blessed is the man who can recognize him in all his disguises. One moment he is a glass of fresh water, the next your son bouncing on your knees or an enchanting woman, or perhaps merely a morning walk.

—Nikos Kazantzakis

In whatever direction you turn, you will see God coming to meet you; nothing is void of him, he himself fills all his work.

—Seneca the Younger

When you find that your soul, your heart, your wisp of inspiration, every speck of the vast blue sky and its shining star-blossoms, the mountains, the earth, the whipporwill, and the bluebells are all tied together with one cord of rhythm, one cord of joy, one cord of unity, one cord of Spirit, then you shall know that all are but waves in His cosmic sea.

—Paramahansa Yogananda

The mystics simply open their souls to the oncoming wave.

—HENRI BERGSON

Who have all the powers of their soul in harmony, and the same loving mind for all; who find joy in the good of all beings—they reach in truth my very self.

—BHAGAVAD GITA

When one knows thee, then alien there is none, then no door is shut. Oh, grant me my prayer that I may never lose the touch of the one in the play of the many.

—RABINDRANATH TAGORE

I see God in every human being. When I wash the leper's wounds I feel I am nursing the Lord himself.

—MOTHER TERESA

When a man sees that the God in himself is the same God in all that is, he hurts not himself by hurting others: then he goes indeed to the highest Path.

—BHAGAVAD GITA

On the basis of the belief that all human beings share the same divine nature, we have a very strong ground, a very powerful reason, to believe that it is possible for each of us to develop a genuine sense of equanimity toward all beings.

—DALAI LAMA

We were born to make manifest the glory of God that is within us. It's not just in some of us, it's in every one. And as we let our own light shine, we unconsciously give other people permission to do the same.

—NELSON MANDELA

If I could persuade myself that I should find Him in a Himalayan cave, I would proceed there immediately. But I know that I cannot find Him apart from humanity.

—MOHANDAS K. GANDHI

A religious man is a person who holds God and man in one thought at one time, at all times, who suffers harm done to others, whose greatest passion is compassion, whose greatest strength is love and defiance of despair.

—ABRAHAM JOSHUA HESCHEL

If you are conscious that you are wanting in [fraternal] charity, although you may feel devotion and sweetness and a short absorption in the prayer of quiet—which makes you think you have obtained the union with God—believe me you have not yet reached it. Beg our Lord to grant you perfect love for your neighbour, and leave the rest to Him. He will give you more than you know how to desire.

—TERESA OF AVILA

# Mending
# the Cosmos

In the secret of my heart I am in perpetual quarrel with God that he should allow such things [as the death and destruction at the start of World War II] to go on.

—MOHANDAS K. GANDHI

Mankind must remember that peace is not God's gift to his creatures; peace is our gift to each other.

—ELIE WIESEL

Whatever good befalls a man, it is from Allah; whatever ill befalls a man, it is his own doing.

—QUR'AN

There is only one way in which one can endure man's inhumanity to man and that is to try, in one's own life, to exemplify man's humanity to man.

—ALAN PATON

Life is short and we have never too much time for gladdening the hearts of those who are traveling the dark journey with us. Oh, be swift to love, make haste to be kind!

—Henri Amiel

The law of our life can be summed up in the axiom "be what you are."

—Thomas Merton

God loves to see in me, not his servant, but himself who serves all.

—Rabindranath Tagore

Whoever surrenders his face to God and performs good deeds, he verily has grasped the surest handle, and unto God is the sequel of all things.

—Qur'an

The most acceptable service of God is doing good to man.

—Benjamin Franklin

For mortal to aid mortal—this is god; and this is the road to eternal glory.

—Pliny the Elder

I will spend my heaven doing good on earth.

—Thérèse de Lisieux

Treat others with the mind of giving, and practice doing works that have no reward.

—Master Baek

A gift is pure when it is given from the heart to the right person at the right time and at the right place, and when we expect nothing in return.

—BHAGAVAD GITA

No sacrifice is worth the name unless it is a joy. Sacrifice and a long face go ill together.

—MOHANDAS K. GANDHI

The Holy Spirit rests only on him who has a joyous heart.

—TALMUD

Anticipate charity by preventing poverty; assist the reduced fellowman, either by a considerable gift, or a sum of money, or by teaching him a trade, or by putting him in the way of business, so that he may earn an honest livelihood, and not be forced to the dreadful alternative of holding out his hand for charity. This is the highest step and the summit of charity's golden ladder.

—MAIMONIDES

The greatest charity is to enable the poor to earn a living.

—TALMUD

Charity never humiliated him who profited from it, nor ever bound him by the chains of gratitude, since it was not to him but to God that the gift was made.

—ANTOINE DE SAINT-EXUPÉRY

What you do not want done to yourself do not do to others.

—CONFUCIUS

Do not do unto others as you would they should do unto you. Their tastes may not be the same.

—GEORGE BERNARD SHAW

If I knew for a certainty that a man was coming to my house with the conscious design of doing me good, I should run for my life.

—HENRY DAVID THOREAU

Do unto others as though you were the others.

—ELBERT HUBBARD

What is hateful to you do not do to your neighbor. That is the whole Torah. The rest is commentary.

—HILLEL

A man, to be greatly good, must imagine intensely and comprehensively; he must put himself in the place of another and of many others; the pains and pleasures of his species must become his own.

—PERCY BYSSHE SHELLEY

Compassion is the desire that moves the individual self to widen the scope of its self-concern to embrace the whole of the universal self.

—ARNOLD J. TOYNBEE

See everyone as a Buddha. This purifies the mind of ignorance and arrogance.

—MASTER BAEK

Thinking of human beings alone is a bit narrow. To consider that all sentient beings in the universe have been our mother at some point in time opens a space of compassion.

—DALAI LAMA

The Lord lives in the heart of every creature.

—BHAGAVAD GITA

A man is ethical only when life, as such, is sacred to him, that of plants and animals as that of his fellow men, and when he devotes himself helpfully to all life that is in need of help.

—ALBERT SCHWEITZER

All God's creatures are His family; and he is the most beloved of God who doeth most good to God's creatures.

—MUHAMMAD

To feel compassion is to feel that we are in some sort and to some extent responsible for the pain that is being inflicted, that we ought to do something about it.

—ALDOUS HUXLEY

What value has compassion that does not take its object in its arms?

—ANTOINE DE SAINT-EXUPÉRY

We ourselves feel that what we are doing is just a drop in the ocean. But if that drop was not in the ocean, I think the ocean would be less because of that missing drop. I do not agree with the big way of doing things.

—MOTHER TERESA

He who would do good to another must do it
    in Minute Particulars:
General Good is the plea of the scoundrel,
    hypocrite, and flatterer,
For Art and Science cannot exist but in
    minutely organized Particulars.

—WILLIAM BLAKE

The best portion of a good man's life;
His little, nameless, unremembered acts
Of kindness and of love.

—WILLIAM WORDSWORTH

The greatest pleasure I know, is to do a good action by stealth, and to have it found out by accident.

—CHARLES LAMB

A good picture is equivalent to a good deed.

—VINCENT VAN GOGH

Work is love made visible.

—KAHLIL GIBRAN

The most excellent method which I found of going to God was that of *doing my common business* purely for the love of God.

—BROTHER LAWRENCE

Let there be no disappointment when obedience keeps you busy in outward tasks. If it sends you to the kitchen, remember that the Lord walks among the pots and pans.

—TERESA OF AVILA

You can mend the cosmos by anything you do— even eating. Do not imagine that God wants you to eat for mere pleasure or to fill your belly. No, the purpose is mending.... By [saying] a blessing when eating], you bring forth sparks [of holiness] that cleave to your soul.

—KABBALAH

The gratitude ascending from man to God is the supreme transaction between earth and heaven.

—ALBERT SCHWEITZER

Make friends with the angels, who though invisible are always with you.... Often invoke them, constantly praise them, and make good use of their help and assistance in all your temporal and spiritual affairs.

—Francis de Sales

If those around us make mistakes, we can easily offer them our compassion, since God is constantly showering His compassion upon us.

—Sri Chinmoy

It must be said that genuine compassion is not like pity or a feeling that others are somehow lower than you. Rather, with genuine compassion you view others as more important than yourself.

—Dalai Lama

Humility must always be doing its work like a bee making honey in the hive; without humility all will be lost.

—Teresa of Avila

Man is not God's last word: God can still create. If you cannot do His work, He will produce some being who can.

—George Bernard Shaw

And do not say, regarding anything, "I am going to do that tomorrow," but only, "if God will."

—Qur'an

In His will is our peace.

—Dante

Cultivate peace and harmony with all.

—GEORGE WASHINGTON

The greater our awareness regarding the value and effectiveness of other religious traditions, then the deeper will be our respect and reverence toward other religions. This is the proper way for us to promote genuine compassion and a spirit of harmony among the religions of the world.

—DALAI LAMA

Religion is a candle inside a multicolored lantern. Everyone looks through a particular color, but the candle is always there.

—MUHAMMAD NAGUIB

You will not enter Paradise until you have faith, and you will not complete your faith until you love one another.

—MUHAMMAD

Remember God and God's love constantly.

—KABBALAH

Think of God more frequently than you breathe.

—EPICTETUS

All power renounced but that of love; the gentleness in all of us redeemed and exalted: the peaceable kingdom.

—THEODORE ROSZAK

May innumerable oceans of realms be filled
With the melodious roar of the profound
　　secret....
May the light of the Buddhas' wisdom be
　　revealed....
May all the world be filled with peace and
　　happiness.

—Tibetan Prayers for World Peace,
KARMA TRIYANA DHARMACHAKRA

Prayer is the way to both the heart of God and the heart of the world.

—HENRI J. M. NOUWEN

Prayer is not an old woman's idle amusement. Properly understood and applied, it is the most potent instrument of action.

—MOHANDAS K. GANDHI

I pray every single second of my life—not on my knees but with my work. Work and worship are one with me.

—Susan B. Anthony

Pray inwardly, even if you do not enjoy it. It does good, though you feel nothing. Yes, even though you think you are doing nothing.

—Julian of Norwich

This conversion into prayer of our everyday joys, sorrows, hopes and desires is at first a conscious labor, but after a while it becomes second nature, so that converse with God becomes inextricably and wonderfully woven into the fabric of our lives.

—Sheila Cassidy

It has been said that prayer is perfect when he who prays remembers not that he is praying.

—PETER OF ALCÁNTARA

The path of spirituality is a knife-edge between abysses.

—ALDOUS HUXLEY

The beauty of the world...has two edges, one of laughter, one of anguish, cutting the heart asunder.

—VIRGINIA WOOLF

Doubt is part of all religion. All the religious thinkers were doubters.

—ISAAC BASHEVIS SINGER

Suppose the world were only one of God's jokes, would you work any the less to make it a good one instead of a bad one?

—George Bernard Shaw

What is faith but a kind of betting or speculation after all? It should be, "I bet that my Redeemer liveth."

—Samuel Butler

Cleave ever to the sunnier side of doubt.

—Alfred, Lord Tennyson

I have not lost faith in God. I have moments of anger and protest. Sometimes I've been closer to him for that reason.

—Elie Wiesel

When a contradiction is impossible to resolve except by a lie, then we know that it is really a door.

—Simone Weil

My Lord God, I have no idea where I am going. I do not see the road ahead of me. I cannot know for certain where it will end. Nor do I really know myself, and the fact that I think that I am following your will does not mean that I am actually doing so. But I believe that the desire to please you does in fact please you. And I hope I have that desire in all that I am doing. I hope that I will never do anything apart from that desire. And I know that if I do this you will lead me by the right road though I may know nothing about it. Therefore will I trust you always though I may seem to be lost and in the shadow of death. I will not fear, for you are ever with me, and you will never leave me to face my perils alone.

—Thomas Merton

Have I not commanded thee? Be strong and of a good courage; be not afraid, neither be thou dismayed; for the Lord thy God is with thee whithersoever thou goest.

—JOSHUA 1:9

All shall be well, and all shall be well, and all manner of thing shall be well.

—JULIAN OF NORWICH

All manner of thing shall be well
By the purification of the motive
In the ground of our beseeching.

—T. S. ELIOT

With upright body, head and neck lead the mind and its powers into the heart; and the OM of Brahman will then be thy boat with which to cross the rivers of fear.

—BHAGAVAD GITA

It is a common experience that a problem difficult at night is resolved in the morning after the committee of sleep has worked on it.

—JOHN STEINBECK

Sleep is the best meditation.

—DALAI LAMA

We have forgotten the age-old fact that God speaks chiefly through dreams and visions.

—CARL JUNG

In the summer of A.D. 1936, in a time of physical sickness and spiritual travail, he [i.e., Toynbee, referring to himself in the third person] dreamed, during a spell of sleep in a wakeful night, that he was clasping the foot of the crucifix hanging over the high altar of the Abbey of Ampleforth and was hearing a voice saying to him *Amplexus expecta* ("Cling and wait").

—ARNOLD J. TOYNBEE

Have patience with everything unresolved in your heart and try to love *the questions themselves....* Don't search for the answers, which could not be given to you now, because you would not be able to live them. And the point is, to live everything. *Live* the questions now. Perhaps, then, someday far in the future, you will gradually, without even noticing it, live your way into the answer.

—RAINER MARIA RILKE

Patient and regular practice is the whole secret of spiritual realization. Do not be in a hurry in spiritual life. Do your utmost, and leave the rest to God.

—SWAMI SHIVANANDA

If a word of a great mystic, or some one of his imitators, finds an echo in one or another of us, may it not be that there is a mystic dormant within us, merely waiting for an occasion to awake?

—HENRI BERGSON